MW00744989

Table of Contents

"Baked" Nacho Dip in Bread Bowl

MAKES 8 TO 10 SERVINGS | PREP: 5 minutes **START TO FINISH:** 20 minutes

1 round bread loaf (1½ to 2 pounds)

1½ cups (6 ounces) shredded Cheddar cheese

1 package (8 ounces) cream cheese, softened

1 cup plain yogurt

1 cup ORTEGA® Garden Vegetable Salsa

2 green onions, diced

3 tablespoons ORTEGA® Taco Sauce, any variety

12 ORTEGA® Taco Shells, broken into bite-sized pieces

SLICE top off bread. Pull out center of bread to create bowl. Slice top and removed bread into bite-sized pieces. Cover; set aside.

COMBINE Cheddar cheese, cream cheese, yogurt, salsa, green onions and taco sauce in large microwave-safe bowl; mix well. Cover bowl; microwave on HIGH (100% power) 5 minutes, stirring halfway through to heat evenly.

POUR dip into bread bowl. Cover; microwave on HIGH 4 minutes longer; stirring halfway through to heat evenly. Serve hot dip with bite-sized bread and taco pieces.

TIPS

For tasty crudités, add your favorite vegetables around the bread bowl.

You can also make this dip without the bread bowl. Just pour the prepared dip into a small (1-quart) slow cooker to keep it warm. Serve with bite-sized taco pieces.

Perfect for Parties

Chicken Fundido

MAKES 4 SERVINGS | PREP: 10 minutes **START TO FINISH:** 20 minutes

1 tablespoon olive oil

1 cup chopped onion

1 cup diced cooked chicken

1 cup ORTEGA® salsa, any variety

1 can (4 ounces) ORTEGA® Diced Jalapeño Peppers, drained

1½ cups (6 ounces) Monterey Jack cheese

1 package (10-count) ORTEGA® Tostada Shells

PREHEAT oven to 350°F.

HEAT olive oil in medium skillet over medium-low heat. Add onions; cook and stir 4 minutes or until translucent. Stir in chicken, salsa and jalapeños.

SPOON mixture into 2-cup gratin dish* or 6- or 7-inch ovenproof skillet. Spread cheese evenly over top.

BAKE 10 minutes or until cheese is melted and bubbly.

BREAK tostada shells into large pieces. Serve with fundido for dipping.

A gratin dish is a shallow ovenproof ceramic dish. If you don't have a gratin dish, substitute an 8-inch glass pie pan.

TIP

Have the entire family dig into the fundido for a fun dinner. For a more colorful presentation, garnish the fundido with fresh chopped tomatoes and cilantro.

Perfect for Parties

Guacamole Sliders

MAKES 12 SMALL BURGERS | **PREP:** 10 minutes **START TO FINISH:** 20 minutes

- 1 ripe avocado
- 1 tablespoon ORTEGA® Fire-Roasted Diced Green Chiles
- 1 tablespoon chopped cilantro
- 1 tablespoon lime juice
- ⅛ teaspoon salt
- 1 pound lean ground beef
- 1 tablespoon water
- 1 cup ORTEGA® Garden Vegetable Salsa, Medium, divided
- 12 dinner rolls

CUT avocado in half and remove pit. Scoop out avocado with spoon and place in small bowl. Add chiles, cilantro, lime juice and salt. Gently mash with fork until blended; set aside.

COMBINE beef, water and ½ cup salsa in medium bowl. Form mixture into 12 small round balls. Flatten slightly.

GRILL or pan-fry burgers about 3 minutes. Turn over and flatten with spatula. Cook 4 minutes longer or until desired doneness.

CUT each roll in half. Fill with 1 tablespoon remaining salsa, 1 burger and 1 heaping tablespoon guacamole. Serve immediately.

TIP
Try using a panini press or similar double-sided grill to cook the sliders even faster.

Perfect for Parties

Hot Beef n' Cheddar Chili Dip with Fiesta Flats Scoops

MAKES AT LEAST 24 SERVINGS | **PREP:** 5 minutes **START TO FINISH:** 15 minutes

1 pound ground beef

1 onion, diced (about 1 cup)

1 cup ORTEGA® Thick & Chunky Salsa, Medium

1 packet (1.25 ounces) ORTEGA® 40% Less Sodium Taco Seasoning Mix

4 cups shredded Cheddar cheese

2 boxes (12 shells each) ORTEGA® Fiesta Flats Flat Bottom Taco Shells

BROWN ground beef and onion in large skillet over medium-high heat 6 to 8 minutes, stirring to break up meat. Drain fat.

ADD salsa, taco seasoning mix and ½ cup water. Stir until well combined.

REDUCE heat to low; add half of cheese. Stir until melted. Add remaining cheese. Cook and stir 4 minutes or until melted.

SERVE hot in heatproof bowl with the Fiesta Flats as dipping "scoops."

TIP

Fill Fiesta Flats with Beef N' Cheddar Dip for a great addition to any party.

Perfect for Parties

Ortega® 7-Layer Dip

MAKES 10 TO 12 SERVINGS | **PREP:** 10 minutes **START TO FINISH:** 10 minutes

1 can (16 ounces) ORTEGA® Refried Beans

1 packet (1.25 ounces) ORTEGA® Taco Seasoning Mix

1 container (8 ounces) sour cream

1 container (8 ounces) prepared guacamole

1 cup (4 ounces) shredded Cheddar cheese

1 cup ORTEGA® Salsa, any variety

1 can (4 ounces) ORTEGA® Fire-Roasted Diced Green Chiles

2 large green onions, sliced

Tortilla chips

COMBINE beans and seasoning mix in small bowl. Spread bean mixture in 8-inch square baking dish.

TOP with sour cream, guacamole, cheese, salsa, chiles and green onions, spreading each layer evenly in baking dish. Serve with chips.

NOTE

This dip can be prepared and refrigerated up to 2 hours before serving.

Sweet and Spicy Cocktail Meatballs

MAKES ABOUT 40 MEATBALLS | PREP: 2 minutes **START TO FINISH:** 10 minutes

1 tablespoon vegetable oil

1 pound prepared frozen meatballs

1 pouch (7 ounces) ORTEGA® Cilantro and Green Chile Skillet Sauce

¼ cup grape jelly

3 tablespoons ORTEGA® Diced Jalapeños

Chopped fresh cilantro (optional)

HEAT oil in large skillet over medium heat. Add meatballs and ½ cup water. Cover and heat through 5 minutes to defrost.

REMOVE cover. Add skillet sauce, jelly and jalapeños; cook and stir 4 minutes until sauce begins to thicken.

SERVE in chaffing dish topped with chopped cilantro and toothpicks for easy pick up.

TIP
These meatballs also make a great taco filling.

Perfect for Parties

9

Taco Sliders

MAKES 8 TACOS | PREP: 5 minutes **START TO FINISH:** 30 minutes

- 1 pound lean ground beef
- 1 can (4 ounces) ORTEGA® Fire-Roasted Diced Green Chiles
- 1 packet (1.25 ounces) ORTEGA® 40% Less Sodium Taco Seasoning Mix
- 4 slices American cheese, cut into quarters
- 8 ORTEGA® Taco Shells, any variety
- 1 cup shredded iceberg lettuce
- 1 tomato, sliced
- 16 dill pickle chips
- ¼ cup mustard
- ¼ cup ORTEGA® Taco Sauce, hot

COMBINE ground beef, chiles and seasoning mix in medium bowl; mix well. Form into 16 small patties.

HEAT medium skillet over medium heat. Add patties; cook 4 minutes on each side or until done. Top each patty with cheese; cook 2 minutes or until cheese is melted.

FILL taco shells evenly with lettuce, tomato, 2 cooked patties and 2 pickle chips. Combine mustard and taco sauce; serve with tacos.

TIP

For a delicious alternative, try making these with warmed ORTEGA® Flour Soft Tortillas, and wrap up the filling before serving.

Perfect for Parties

Taco Tempura with Tangy Dipping Sauce

MAKES 6 SERVINGS | PREP: 10 minutes **START TO FINISH:** 15 minutes

1 cup tempura batter

1 packet (1.25 ounces) ORTEGA® Taco Seasoning Mix

¼ cup sour cream

¼ cup ORTEGA® Green Taco Sauce

1 cup vegetable oil

1 onion, cut into quarters and separated into petals

1 large carrot, cut thinly on the bias

1 yellow bell pepper, sliced into strips

1 cup broccoli florets

COMBINE tempura batter, taco seasoning mix and ¾ cup water in medium bowl. Mix well; allow to sit 5 minutes to thicken slightly.

PREPARE dipping sauce by combining sour cream with green taco sauce.

HEAT oil in large skillet over medium heat. Dredge each vegetable slice into taco-tempura batter, shaking to remove excess batter. Drop vegetables in batches in hot oil; cook 3 minutes, turning over and continuing another 3 minutes. Remove and drain on paper towel.

SERVE taco-tempura vegetables immediately with dipping sauce.

TIP

Try dipping peeled and deveined shrimp into the batter as well.

Perfect for Parties

Angry Clam Chowder

MAKES 8 SERVINGS | **PREP:** 5 minutes **START TO FINISH:** 25 minutes

3 bacon slices, diced

1 onion, diced (about 1 cup)

1 stalk celery, diced

2 carrots, peeled and diced (about 1 cup)

1 can (7 ounces) ORTEGA® Diced Jalapeños

1 jar (16 ounces) ORTEGA® Salsa, Medium

1 pound minced clams

2 cups red potatoes, diced

BROWN bacon in large stockpot over medium heat 4 minutes or until crispy. Push bacon aside; add onion, celery, carrots and jalapeños. Toss to coat with bacon and continue to cook 5 minutes or until vegetables become wilted.

ADD salsa, 2 salsa jars of water and clams. Stir to combine; add potatoes. Reduce heat to low; cover and cook 15 minutes until the potatoes are cooked and soup is slightly thickened.

TIP

For an even spicier chowder, add ORTEGA® Taco Sauce. For more texture, sprinkle with crushed ORTEGA® Corn Taco Shells.

Simmering Soups

Black Bean and Bacon Soup

MAKES 6 TO 8 SERVINGS | PREP: 5 minutes **START TO FINISH:** 30 minutes

5 strips bacon, sliced

1 medium onion, diced

2 tablespoons ORTEGA® Fire-Roasted Diced Green Chiles

2 cans (15 ounces each) ORTEGA® Black Beans, undrained

4 cups chicken broth

½ cup ORTEGA® Taco Sauce, any variety

½ cup sour cream

4 ORTEGA® Yellow Corn Taco Shells, crumbled

COOK bacon in large pot over medium heat 5 minutes or until crisp. Add onion and chiles. Cook 5 minutes or until onion begins to brown. Stir in beans, broth and taco sauce. Bring to a boil. Reduce heat to low. Simmer 20 minutes.

PURÉE half of soup in food processor until smooth (or use immersion blender in pot). Return puréed soup to pot and stir to combine. Serve with dollop of sour cream and crumbled taco shells.

NOTE

For a less chunky soup, purée the entire batch and cook an additional 15 minutes.

Simmering Soups

Chilled Avocado Soup

MAKES 4 TO 6 SERVINGS | PREP: 15 minutes **START TO FINISH:** 15 minutes

- 4 ripe avocados
- 1 cup chicken broth
- ¾ cup sour cream
- 3 green onions, chopped
- 2 tablespoons ORTEGA® Taco Sauce, hot
- 1 jar (8 ounces) ORTEGA® Green Taco Sauce
- 2 cups water
- Juice of 1 lime
- ½ teaspoon salt
- Additional ORTEGA® Green Taco Sauce (optional)
- ORTEGA® Tostada Shells, broken in half (optional)

CUT avocados in half and remove pits. Scrape avocado flesh into food processor or blender.

ADD broth, sour cream, green onions and 2 tablespoons taco sauce. Process using on/off pulsing action until ingredients are finely chopped.

ADD 1 jar taco sauce, water,* lime juice and salt. Pulse until evenly mixed, stopping occasionally to scrape sides of bowl with rubber spatula. Process 2 minutes or until smooth. Refrigerate at least 2 hours or until chilled before serving.

GARNISH with 1 tablespoon additional taco sauce and serve with tostada shells, if desired.

Pour some of the water into the emptied jar and shake to release any trapped sauce; add to food processor.

Simmering Soups

Chipotle Carrot Soup

MAKES 6 SERVINGS | PREP: 10 minutes **START TO FINISH:** 30 minutes

1 tablespoon olive oil

1 cup diced onions

1 pound carrots, peeled, chopped

1 packet (1.25 ounces) ORTEGA® Chipotle Taco Seasoning Mix

4 cups chicken broth

1 cup water

2 tablespoons butter

6 ORTEGA® Yellow Corn Taco Shells, broken

HEAT oil in large saucepan over medium-high heat. Add onions; cook and stir 3 minutes or until softened.

ADD carrots and seasoning mix; toss until evenly coated. Stir in broth and water. Bring to a boil. Reduce heat to medium-low. Cover; simmer 20 minutes or until carrots are tender.

POUR soup into blender or food processor in two batches. Pulse several times until well combined. Pour back into saucepan. Add butter and reheat before serving.

TOP each serving with taco shells.

Simmering Soups

Easy Salsa Soup

MAKES 6 SERVINGS | PREP: 5 minutes **START TO FINISH:** 20 minutes

2 jars (16 ounces each) ORTEGA® Original Salsa

1 package (8 ounces) cream cheese

4 ORTEGA® Taco Shells, crumbled

COMBINE salsa and cream cheese in large saucepan. Cook and stir over medium heat 5 minutes or until cream cheese is melted. Reduce heat to medium-low. Cook 5 minutes.

POUR into blender or food processor in two batches; pulse several times until well combined. Return to saucepan. Cook over low heat 5 minutes. Serve with crumbled shells.

TIP

For a fun party appetizer, serve the soup in small espresso cups or shot glasses. Tell guests to enjoy their "Salsa Soup Shooters."

Firecracker Tortilla Soup

MAKES 6 SERVINGS | **PREP:** 10 minutes **START TO FINISH:** 30 minutes

- 2 tablespoons olive oil
- 1 large onion, diced
- 1 teaspoon POLANER® Chopped Garlic
- 1 teaspoon ground cumin
- 1 cup ORTEGA® Thick & Chunky Salsa
- 1 packet (1.25 ounces) ORTEGA® Chipotle Taco Seasoning Mix
- 6 cups chicken broth
- 10 ORTEGA® Yellow Corn Taco Shells or Whole Grain Corn Taco Shells, divided
- ¼ cup sour cream

HEAT oil in large saucepot over medium heat until hot. Add onion, garlic and cumin. Cook and stir 5 minutes or until onion is tender. Stir in salsa and taco seasoning mix. Add broth and bring to a boil. Reduce heat to low.

BREAK up 8 taco shells; stir into soup. Cook over low heat 15 minutes.

PURÉE soup in blender or food processor in batches until smooth (or use immersion blender in saucepot). Return puréed soup to saucepot and stir to combine. Serve with additional crumbled taco shells and top with dollop of sour cream.

TIP

Garnish with chopped green onions, cilantro, shredded Cheddar cheese or ORTEGA® Guacamole Style Dip.

Roasted Corn and Chicken Soup

MAKES 8 SERVINGS | PREP: 15 minutes **START TO FINISH:** 30 minutes

4 tablespoons olive oil, divided

1 can (15 ounces) yellow corn, drained

1 can (15 ounces) white corn, drained

1 onion, diced

3 tablespoons ORTEGA® Fire-Roasted Diced Green Chiles

½ of 1½- to 2-pound cooked rotisserie chicken, bones removed and meat shredded

1 packet (1.25 ounces) ORTEGA® 40% Less Sodium Taco Seasoning Mix

4 cups chicken broth

4 ORTEGA® Yellow Corn Taco Shells, crumbled

HEAT 2 tablespoons oil over medium heat in large skillet until hot. Add corn. Cook 8 minutes or until browned; stir often to prevent corn from burning. Add remaining 2 tablespoons oil, onion and chiles. Cook and stir 3 minutes longer.

TRANSFER mixture to large pot. Stir in shredded chicken. Add seasoning mix and toss to combine. Stir in chicken broth and bring to a boil. Reduce heat to low. Simmer 15 minutes. Serve with crumbled taco shells.

TIP

To make sure the canned corn is well drained, press excess water out with a paper towel.

Simmering Soups

Turkey Taco Soup

MAKES 6 SERVINGS | **PREP:** 5 minutes **START TO FINISH:** 30 minutes

1 tablespoon olive oil

½ cup diced onion

1 tablespoon POLANER® Minced Garlic

1 pound ground turkey

1 tablespoon ORTEGA® Chili Seasoning Mix

½ teaspoon salt

½ teaspoon black pepper

3 cups chicken broth

1 can (16 ounces) ORTEGA® Refried Beans

1 tablespoon ORTEGA® Fire-Roasted Diced Green Chiles

1 cup shredded lettuce

½ cup chopped tomato

4 ORTEGA® Yellow Corn Taco Shells, crumbled

HEAT oil in large saucepan over medium heat. Add onion and garlic; cook and stir 5 minutes. Stir in turkey, chili seasoning mix, salt and pepper. Cook and stir 5 minutes to break up turkey.

ADD broth, beans and chiles; stir until beans are mixed in well. Cook over medium heat 10 minutes.

DIVIDE soup among 6 bowls. Divide lettuce among bowls, and stir in to wilt lettuce slightly. Top each serving with chopped tomato and crumbled taco shells.

TIP

For additional flavor variations, use lean ground beef or ground chicken in this soup.

Cheesy Enchilada Shrimp

MAKES ABOUT 35 SHRIMP | PREP: 5 minutes **START TO FINISH:** 20 minutes

1 can (10 ounces)
      ORTEGA® Enchilada
      Sauce, Mild

1 pound large shrimp,
      peeled

2 cups (8 ounces)
      shredded
      mozzarella cheese

PREHEAT oven to 400°F.

POUR half of enchilada sauce in bottom of 8- to 10-inch ovenproof serving dish. Top with peeled shrimp in single layer. Pour remainder of enchilada sauce over top of shrimp. Sprinkle with cheese to cover.

BAKE 12 minutes or until cheese is melted and sauce begins to bubble. Serve warm with toothpicks.

TIP
Use these for a filling for ORTEGA® Fiesta Flats.

Chicken Salsa Sandwiches

MAKES 4 SANDWICHES | **PREP:** 5 minutes **START TO FINISH:** 10 minutes

2   cups cooked chicken breast, cut into ½-inch dice

¼   cup mayonnaise

¼   cup ORTEGA® Thick & Chunky Salsa, medium

2   tablespoons drained ORTEGA® Fire-Roasted Diced Green Chiles

8   slices rye bread

½   cup ORTEGA® Guacamole Style Dip

1   tomato, sliced

4   leaves Boston lettuce

COMBINE chicken, mayonnaise, salsa and chiles in medium bowl; mix well.

TOAST bread; spread with guacamole dip. Divide chicken mixture evenly among 4 slices. Add tomato and lettuce; close sandwiches with remaining bread slices.

TIP

For a sweet and spicy sandwich, use leftover turkey instead of the chicken, and add some canned cranberry sauce to the filling mixture.

Chicken Taco Salad Wraps

MAKES 4 SERVINGS (3 WRAPS EACH)
PREP: 15 minutes **START TO FINISH:** 30 minutes

1 ripe large avocado, pitted, peeled and diced

¾ cup peeled and diced jicama

2 teaspoons lime juice

2 tablespoons vegetable oil

1 pound boneless skinless chicken breasts, cut into strips

1 packet (1.25 ounces) ORTEGA® Taco Seasoning Mix

¾ cup water

8 ORTEGA® Taco Shells, any variety, coarsely crushed

12 large Bibb lettuce leaves

½ cup (2 ounces) shredded Mexican cheese blend

¼ cup chopped fresh cilantro

1 jar (8 ounces) ORTEGA® Taco Sauce, any variety

COMBINE avocado, jicama and lime juice in small bowl; stir well. Set aside.

HEAT oil in large skillet over medium-high heat. Add chicken strips; cook and stir 4 to 6 minutes or until chicken is no longer pink.

STIR in seasoning mix and water. Bring to a boil. Reduce heat to low; cook 2 to 3 minutes or until mixture is thickened, stirring occasionally. Remove from heat.

MICROWAVE crushed taco shells on HIGH (100% power) 1 minute.

SPOON ⅓ cup chicken filling onto each lettuce leaf; layer with taco shells, avocado mixture, cheese and cilantro. Wrap lettuce around filling and serve with taco sauce.

Chipotle Chicken Taco Cones

MAKES 8 CONES | **PREP:** 10 minutes **START TO FINISH:** 20 minutes

1 tablespoon olive oil

1 onion, diced

1 pound ground chicken

¾ cup water

1 packet (1.25 ounces) ORTEGA® Chipotle Taco Seasoning Mix

1 can (16 ounces) ORTEGA® Refried Beans

8 (8-inch) ORTEGA® Flour Soft Tortillas

1 cup shredded lettuce

1 cup diced tomatoes

1 cup (4 ounces) shredded Cheddar cheese

HEAT olive oil in medium skillet over medium heat. Add onion; cook and stir 3 minutes or until translucent. Add ground chicken; cook and stir 5 minutes or until browned. Stir in water and seasoning mix. Remove from heat.

WARM refried beans in saucepan or in microwave.

WRAP tortillas in lightly moistened paper towels. Microwave on HIGH (100% power) 20 to 30 seconds, or until pliable.

FOLD tortilla in half; spread with refried beans. Form tortilla into cone shape;* press to adhere outside corner with refried beans.

FILL cones with chicken mixture, lettuce, tomatoes and Cheddar cheese.

To form cone, lay tortilla on work surface. Holding one pointed end down, grasp other end and bring point to round edge, twisting point under slightly. Curl opposite end around outside of cone and press to adhere with refried beans.

Club Quesadillas

MAKES 4 SERVINGS | PREP: 10 minutes **START TO FINISH:** 20 minutes

Nonstick cooking spray

½ cup ORTEGA® Refried Beans

6 (8-inch) ORTEGA® Flour Soft Tortillas

2 tomatoes, sliced

½ cup (2 ounces) shredded Cheddar cheese

6 slices deli turkey meat

6 slices cooked bacon

½ cup shredded iceberg lettuce

SPRAY large skillet with cooking spray over medium heat.

SPREAD ¼ of the beans onto tortilla and place in skillet. Top with 3 to 4 slices tomato, ¼ of the cheese, another tortilla and another layer of beans. Add 3 slices turkey, 3 slices bacon, sprinkle of cheese and lettuce. Top with another tortilla.

HEAT 4 minutes, gently flip the entire tortilla, smashing down with spatula. Heat the other side 5 minutes or until cheese is melted and tortillas have browned. Remove from pan and cut into 6 pieces.

REPEAT with remaining ingredients to create a second club quesadilla.

TIP
Serve with broken taco shells and guacamole for a great meal.

Weeknight Dinners

Crab and Scallion Quesadillas

MAKES 5 SERVINGS | **PREP:** 10 minutes **START TO FINISH:** 20 minutes

8 ounces pasteurized crabmeat

¾ cup cream cheese, softened

4 green onions (white and green parts), diced

Zest of 1 lime

1 ORTEGA® Soft Taco Kit—includes 10 flour soft tortillas, 1 packet (1.25 ounces) taco seasoning mix and 1 packet (3 ounces) taco sauce

Nonstick cooking spray

1 tomato, diced

¼ cup chopped cilantro

½ cup sour cream

COMBINE crabmeat, cream cheese, green onions, lime zest, and half of seasoning mix from Soft Taco Kit in large mixing bowl.

HEAT large skillet over medium heat and spray with nonstick cooking spray. Spread about 1 teaspoon taco sauce onto flour tortilla from Soft Taco Kit. Spread about ¼ cup of crab mixture over sauce. Place tortilla-side-down into hot skillet and top with another tortilla. Cook about 4 minutes or until bottom of tortilla is browned. Spray top tortilla with nonstick cooking spray and turn over. Cook another 4 minutes. Repeat with remaining quesadillas. (Cook two at a time if skillet is large enough.)

CUT quesadillas into quarters and top with tomato, cilantro and sour cream to serve.

NOTE

Place cooked quesadillas in preheated 200°F oven and cover to keep warm.

Double Trouble Tacos

MAKES 8 TACOS | PREP: 10 minutes **START TO FINISH:** 25 minutes

1 pound ground beef

1 ORTEGA® Grande Taco Dinner Kit— includes 12 hard taco shells, 8 flour soft tortillas, 2 packets (3 ounces) taco sauce and 1 packet (2 ounces) taco seasoning mix

1 pound cooked chicken breast, shredded

1 can (16 ounces) ORTEGA® Refried Beans

1 tomato, diced

2 cups shredded lettuce

1 cup (4 ounces) shredded Cheddar cheese

BROWN ground beef in large skillet over medium heat 6 to 8 minutes, stirring to break up meat. Drain fat. Add taco seasoning mix from Grande Taco Dinner Kit and ¾ cup water. Mix and set aside.

HEAT chicken in second skillet, adding pouch of taco sauce from Dinner Kit.

SPREAD beans onto flour tortilla. Place yellow corn taco shell inside the flour tortilla. Add ground beef and shredded chicken mixture topped with diced tomatoes, lettuce and cheese.

TIP

Feel free to replace the ground beef with ground chicken for a Double Trouble Chicken Taco.

Fiesta Ravioli

MAKES 4 TO 6 SERVINGS | PREP: 5 minutes **START TO FINISH:** 20 minutes

1 tablespoon olive oil

½ cup diced onion

½ cup diced carrots

½ cup diced red bell pepper

1 jar (16 ounces) ORTEGA® Thick & Chunky Salsa, medium

1 can (4 ounces) ORTEGA® Fire-Roasted Diced Green Chiles

1 pound frozen cheese-filled ravioli

½ cup (2 ounces) shredded Cheddar cheese

Chopped fresh cilantro (optional)

BRING large pot of salted water to a boil. Meanwhile, heat oil in medium skillet over medium heat until hot.

ADD onion, carrots and bell pepper to skillet; cook and stir 4 to 5 minutes or until carrots are soft. Add salsa and chiles; cook and stir 5 minutes or until slightly thickened.

COOK ravioli in boiling water according to package directions. Drain; transfer to serving bowl. Top with sauce mixture and sprinkle with cheese. Top with cilantro before serving, if desired.

TIP

Chopped cilantro adds color and authentic Mexican flavor, so keep some on hand to garnish any Mexican dish.

Loco Lobster Rolls

MAKES 4 SANDWICHES | PREP: 10 minutes **START TO FINISH:** 15 minutes

- 1 cup cooked lobster meat, chopped
- ¼ teaspoon celery salt
- 1 stalk celery, diced
- ¼ cup mayonnaise
- 2 tablespoons ORTEGA® Taco Sauce, Medium
- 2 tablespoons ORTEGA® Fire-Roasted Diced Green Chiles
- ½ cup ORTEGA® Black Beans, drained
- 1 packet (1 ounce) ORTEGA® Fish Taco Seasoning Mix
- 4 top-cut or regular hot dog rolls
- 2 tablespoons butter
- 1 cup shredded iceberg lettuce

COMBINE lobster meat, celery salt, celery, mayonnaise, taco sauce, chiles, beans and fish taco seasoning mix in medium bowl. Stir well to combine.

HEAT large skillet over medium heat. Open hot dog rolls and spread butter on inside of each. Lay the rolls flat, face down in the skillet and brown, 4 minutes.

SERVE lobster mixture and shredded lettuce on warmed roll.

TIP

Substitute cooked shrimp for lobster meat to make an excellent shrimp roll.

Weeknight Dinners

Mexican Mongolian Beef

MAKES 4 SERVINGS | **PREP:** 10 minutes **START TO FINISH:** 25 minutes

⅓ cup ORTEGA® Taco Sauce, any variety

⅓ cup hoisin sauce

1 teaspoon ground ginger

1 pound sirloin steak

1 tablespoon cornstarch

2 tablespoons olive oil

1 large onion, sliced

1 to 2 cups cooked vegetables, such as carrots, broccoli or green beans (optional)

Hot cooked rice

4 green onions, sliced

1 tablespoon sesame seeds

COMBINE taco sauce, hoisin sauce and ginger in small bowl; mix well. Set aside.

CUT steak diagonally against the grain into thin slices. Place in medium bowl; toss with cornstarch until evenly coated.

HEAT oil in large skillet over medium heat until hot. Add onion; cook and stir 3 to 4 minutes or until onion is translucent.

ADD steak; cook and stir 5 minutes or until meat is browned. Add sauce mixture and vegetables, if desired; cook and stir 2 minutes or until heated through.

SERVE over rice. Top evenly with green onions and sesame seeds.

TIP

For more savory flavor, mix any variety of ORTEGA® Original Salsa into the cooked rice before serving with the dish.

Mexican Tortilla Stacks

MAKES 16 SERVINGS | **PREP:** 10 minutes **START TO FINISH:** 20 minutes

½ cup ORTEGA® Salsa, any variety, divided

½ cup finely chopped cooked chicken

¼ cup sour cream

8 (8-inch) ORTEGA® Flour Soft Tortillas

½ cup prepared guacamole

⅓ cup ORTEGA® Refried Beans

6 tablespoons (1½ ounces) shredded Cheddar cheese

Additional sour cream and chopped cilantro (optional)

HEAT oven to 350°F. Mix ¼ cup salsa, chicken and ¼ cup sour cream in small bowl.

PLACE 2 tortillas on ungreased cookie sheet; spread each with salsa-chicken mixture. Spread 2 more tortillas with guacamole and place on top of salsa-chicken mixture.

MIX refried beans with remaining ¼ cup salsa; spread onto 2 more tortillas and place on top of guacamole. Top each stack with remaining 2 tortillas; sprinkle with cheese.

BAKE 8 to 10 minutes until cheese is melted and filling is hot.

TOP with sour cream and cilantro, if desired. Cut each stack into 8 wedges.

TIP

Prepared guacamole can be found in the refrigerated or frozen food sections at most supermarkets.

Rotisserie Chicken Tacos

MAKES 10 TACOS | **PREP:** 10 minutes **START TO FINISH:** 25 minutes

1 tablespoon olive oil

1 medium onion, diced

3 cups shredded cooked chicken

1 ORTEGA® Soft Taco Kit—includes 10 flour soft tortillas, 1 packet (1.25 ounces) taco seasoning mix and 1 packet (3 ounces) taco sauce

1 cup ORTEGA® Garden Vegetable Salsa

2 tablespoons ORTEGA® Diced Jalapeños

1 cup shredded lettuce

1 cup shredded pepper jack cheese

HEAT oil in medium skillet over medium heat. Add onion; cook and stir 4 minutes or until translucent. Stir in chicken, taco seasoning mix from Soft Taco Kit, salsa and jalapeños. Cook and stir 5 minutes or until heated through.

HEAT soft tacos from Taco Kit according to package instructions. Fill with chicken mixture and garnish with lettuce and cheese. Serve with taco sauce from Taco Kit, if desired.

TIPS

Any remaining filling can be tossed with your favorite greens to make a great lunch salad.

For ease of preparation, purchase a cooked rotisserie chicken from your supermarket's hot deli case.

Salsa Bacon Burgers with Guacamole

MAKES 4 BURGERS | **PREP:** 10 minutes **START TO FINISH:** 25 minutes

1 pound ground beef

1 packet (1.25 ounces) ORTEGA® Taco Seasoning Mix

¼ cup ORTEGA® Salsa, any variety

2 ripe avocados

1 packet (1 ounce) ORTEGA® Guacamole Seasoning Mix

4 hamburger buns

8 slices cooked bacon

COMBINE ground beef, taco seasoning mix and salsa in large mixing bowl. With clean hands, form meat mixture into 4 patties.

CUT avocados in half and remove pits. Scoop out avocado meat and smash in small bowl. Add guacamole seasoning mix. Set aside.

HEAT large skillet over medium heat; cook burgers 5 minutes. Flip burgers and continue to cook another 7 minutes.

PLACE burgers on bottom of buns. Top each burger with 2 slices bacon, dollop of guacamole and top bun.

TIP

Make burgers half the size to create great sliders.

Salsa Crab Cakes with Mexed-Up Tartar Sauce

MAKES 4 TO 6 SERVINGS | **PREP:** 15 minutes **START TO FINISH:** 25 minutes

Tartar Sauce

- ½ cup mayonnaise
- ¼ cup ORTEGA® Original Salsa, any variety
- 2 tablespoons dill pickle relish

Crab Cakes

- 1 pound pasteurized crabmeat, drained
- ¾ cup seasoned bread crumbs
- 1 egg, beaten
- ¼ cup mayonnaise
- ¼ cup ORTEGA® Original Salsa, any variety
- 1 packet (1.25 ounces) ORTEGA® Taco Seasoning Mix or 40% Less Sodium Taco Seasoning Mix
- ½ cup vegetable or canola oil

COMBINE ½ cup mayonnaise, ¼ cup salsa and pickle relish in small bowl; mix well. Refrigerate until ready to use.

COMBINE crabmeat, bread crumbs, egg, ¼ cup mayonnaise, ¼ cup salsa and seasoning mix in medium bowl; mix well. Form into 6 cakes.

HEAT oil in medium saucepan over medium-high heat until hot. Add crab cakes; fry 5 minutes on each side or until golden brown. Serve with tartar sauce.

SERVING SUGGESTION

Serve the crab cakes over a bed of mixed greens with vinaigrette dressing.

Weeknight Dinners

Southwest Buffalo Chicken Tacos

MAKES 4 SERVINGS | PREP: 5 minutes **START TO FINISH:** 10 minutes

3 tablespoons ORTEGA® Taco Sauce, any variety

½ teaspoon cornstarch

7 ounces chunk chicken breast

4 ORTEGA® Whole Grain Corn Taco Shells

1 stalk celery, diced

½ cup crumbled blue cheese

COMBINE taco sauce and cornstarch in small bowl; mix well.

HEAT small skillet over medium heat. Add chicken and taco sauce mixture; stir well. Reduce heat; cook and stir 4 minutes or until mixture has thickened.

DIVIDE filling evenly among taco shells. Top evenly with celery and blue cheese.

Weeknight Dinners

Turkey and all the Fixin' Tacos

MAKES 8 TACOS | PREP: 10 minutes **START TO FINISH:** 15 minutes

- 1 pound ground turkey
- 1 packet (1.25 ounce) ORTEGA® Taco Seasoning Mix
- ¼ cup ORTEGA® Salsa, any variety
- 2 cups prepared mashed potatoes
- ¼ cup shredded Cheddar cheese
- 8 ORTEGA® Yellow Corn Taco Shells
- ½ cup cranberry sauce

HEAT turkey in large skillet over medium heat 5 minutes, stirring to break up meat. Add taco seasoning mix, salsa and ¼ cup water, stirring to combine. Heat through 3 minutes.

COMBINE mashed potatoes and cheese in large bowl; microwave 2 minutes to heat through.

FILL each taco shell with ¼ cup mashed potatoes; top with turkey and dollop of cranberry sauce.

TIP

This recipe makes a great meal by allowing guests to build their own tacos with the ingredients separated in individual bowls. Try adding French fried onions for added crunch.

Weeknight Dinners

Refried Bean and Corn Cakes

MAKES 6 TO 8 SERVINGS | **PREP:** 10 minutes **START TO FINISH:** 20 minutes

1 can (16 ounces) ORTEGA® Refried Beans

1 cup crushed ORTEGA® Taco Shells

1 egg

1 tablespoon ORTEGA® Fire-Roasted Diced Green Chiles

¼ cup vegetable or corn oil

Sour cream (optional)

½ cup ORTEGA® Black Bean & Corn Salsa

Chopped fresh cilantro (optional)

COMBINE refried beans, taco shells, egg and chiles in large mixing bowl; stir well. Let stand 5 minutes.

HEAT oil in large skillet. Drop bean mixture into pan by heaping tablespoonfuls; do not crowd pan. Mash into flat cakes with spatula. Fry cakes about 4 minutes; turn over and fry 4 minutes longer. Drain on paper towels. Cook remaining bean mixture in batches.

SPOON sour cream, if desired, and 1 tablespoon salsa on each cake. Garnish with cilantro, if desired. Serve warm or at room temperature.

TIP

Although the cakes make a delicious side dish, dressed up with sour cream and cilantro, these make a great vegetarian appetizer too!

Zesty Salads & Sides

Chile'd Wedge Salad

MAKES 4 TO 6 SERVINGS | **PREP:** 20 minutes **START TO FINISH:** 20 minutes

1 tablespoon vegetable oil

1 cup chopped onion

1 teaspoon POLANER® Chopped Garlic

1 pound lean ground beef

¾ cup water

1 can (4 ounces) ORTEGA® Fire-Roasted Diced Green Chiles

1 packet (1.25 ounces) ORTEGA® Taco Seasoning Mix or 40% Less Sodium Taco Seasoning Mix

4 to 6 ORTEGA® Yellow Corn Taco Shells, crumbled

1 head iceberg lettuce

1 cup (4 ounces) shredded Cheddar cheese

1 cup blue cheese dressing

HEAT oil in medium skillet over medium heat until hot. Add onion and garlic; cook and stir 3 minutes. Add ground beef; cook and stir 5 minutes or until beef is browned. Drain and discard fat.

ADD water, chiles and seasoning mix; cook and stir 5 minutes or until thickened.

LINE serving plates evenly with taco shells. Cut core from lettuce; cut into wedges and place wedges on taco shells. Top evenly with beef mixture and cheese. Serve immediately with dressing.

TIP

For a spicier dressing, substitute ORTEGA® Salsa for some of the blue cheese dressing; mix with the dressing before serving.

Zesty Salads & Sides

Diced Potatoes and Chorizo

MAKES 6 SERVINGS | PREP: 5 minutes **START TO FINISH:** 25 minutes

1 pound red potatoes, diced

1 tablespoon ORTEGA® Taco Sauce, medium

1 cup chorizo sausage, diced

1 tablespoon oil

2 tablespoons ORTEGA® Diced Jalapeños

PREHEAT oven to 425°F.

TOSS potatoes, taco sauce and sausage in large bowl. Spread in single layer on baking sheet.

BAKE 10 minutes; stir and bake 10 minutes. Remove from oven; toss with oil and jalapeños.

TIP

Add diced onions and bake with potatoes for another version of this great side dish.

Roasted Mexican Corn

MAKES 6 SERVINGS | **PREP:** 5 minutes **START TO FINISH:** 20 minutes

1 bag (16 ounces) frozen corn

2 tablespoons olive oil

½ cup ORTEGA® Thick & Chunky Salsa, any variety

1 can (4 ounces) ORTEGA® Fire-Roasted Diced Green Chiles

Salt and black pepper, to taste

PREHEAT oven to 450°F.

PLACE frozen corn in colander; rinse with cold running water to thaw and shake colander to drain well. Press corn between paper towels to remove most of moisture. Place on large rimmed baking sheet; drizzle with oil.

BAKE 10 minutes or until corn begins to turn golden brown. Transfer to medium bowl.

STIR in salsa and chiles; season with salt and pepper. Serve warm.

TIP

For a great summer side dish, chill the corn before serving. For a hearty salad, add a can of rinsed and drained ORTEGA® Black Beans and serve chilled.

Zesty Salads & Sides

Salsa-Buttered
Corn on the Cob

MAKES 6 SERVINGS | PREP: 5 minutes **START TO FINISH:** 20 minutes

6 ears fresh corn, shucked

4 tablespoons butter, softened

¼ cup ORTEGA® Salsa, any variety

2 tablespoons ORTEGA® Taco Seasoning Mix, or to taste

BRING large pot of water to a boil. Add corn; cook 5 to 10 minutes.

COMBINE butter and salsa in small bowl; mix well. Place seasoning mix in another small bowl. Spread salsa butter onto cooked corn and sprinkle on seasoning mix, to taste.

TIP

For a different side dish, cut the corn off the cob and heat in a skillet with the salsa butter and taco seasoning mix.

Zesty Salads & Sides

Salsa-fied Grilled Vegetable Salad

MAKES 4 SERVINGS | PREP: 5 minutes **START TO FINISH:** 25 minutes

1 large onion, sliced (about 2 cups)

2 cups peeled and thinly sliced eggplant

2 zucchini, sliced into rings

1 fennel bulb, sliced

Salt and black pepper, to taste

1 cup ORTEGA® Salsa, any variety

3 tablespoons ORTEGA® Diced Jalapeños

1 head Boston lettuce

2 tablespoons REGINA® Balsamic Vinegar

GRILL vegetables in large skillet over medium heat 5 minutes on each side. Remove from heat when wilted but still slightly crunchy. Add salt and pepper to taste.

PLACE vegetables in large mixing bowl; toss in salsa and jalapeños. Serve over lettuce drizzled with balsamic vinegar.

TIP

When tomatoes are in season, grill sliced tomatoes for 2 to 3 minutes, then toss with salsa and jalapeños for a quick tomato salad.

Smokin'
Chipotle Coleslaw

MAKES 5 SERVINGS | **PREP:** 5 minutes **START TO FINISH:** 5 minutes

- 1 bag (16 ounces) coleslaw mix
- 1 packet (1.25 ounces) ORTEGA® Chipotle Seasoning Mix
- 1 cup mayonnaise
- ½ cup ORTEGA® Salsa, any variety
- Salt, to taste

TOSS coleslaw mix and chipotle seasoning mix in large bowl. Fold in mayonnaise and salsa until well combined. Season with salt, if desired.

TIP

For an even crunchier salad, try adding sliced radishes to the slaw. Or serve on beef, chicken or turkey tacos for added zest.

Spicy Watermelon Salad

MAKES 4 TO 6 SERVINGS | PREP: 10 minutes **START TO FINISH:** 10 minutes

4 cups watermelon, cut into ½-inch pieces

1 cup cantaloupe, cut into ½-inch pieces

1 cup blueberries

3 tablespoons minced fresh mint leaves

2 tablespoons ORTEGA® Taco Seasoning Mix or 40% Less Sodium Taco Seasoning Mix

COMBINE watermelon, cantaloupe, blueberries, mint and seasoning mix in large bowl; toss well. Chill before serving.

TIP

For an attractive presentation for any occasion, serve the salad in a watermelon bowl. Cut the watermelon in half and hollow out the inside. If desired, cut small, diagonal triangles along the top of the watermelon bowl using a paring knife. Fill with the Spicy Watermelon Salad and chill before serving.

Zesty Salads & Sides

Taco Breaded Zucchini

MAKES 4 SERVINGS | PREP: 5 minutes **START TO FINISH:** 15 minutes

8 ORTEGA® Yellow Corn Taco Shells

1 egg, slightly beaten

1 packet (1.25 ounces) ORTEGA® Taco Seasoning Mix

1 cup all-purpose flour

¼ cup vegetable oil

2 zucchini, sliced into ¼-inch rings

PLACE taco shells in food processor; pulse several minutes until shells are size of large bread crumbs. Pour into shallow pie pan.

BEAT egg in second shallow pie pan. Combine taco seasoning mix and flour in third shallow pie pan.

HEAT oil in large skillet over medium heat.

DREDGE each of zucchini slices first in taco-seasoned flour, shaking off excess. Next, coat with egg and finally in crushed taco shells; set aside. Place zucchini in batches into oil; cook 4 minutes per side. Remove and drain on paper towels.

TIP

Try this preparation technique with onions rings as well.

Zesty Salads & Sides

Taco Fries

MAKES 6 TO 8 SERVINGS | **PREP:** 2 minutes **START TO FINISH:** 17 minutes

1 packet (1.25 ounces)
ORTEGA® Taco
Seasoning Mix

2 pounds frozen
French fries

1 cup ORTEGA® Taco
Sauce, any variety

PREHEAT oven to 450°F.

SPRINKLE seasoning mix over frozen fries;
toss to coat fries evenly.

BAKE fries according to package instructions.
Serve with taco sauce for dipping.

TIP

For smokier flavor, try this recipe with
ORTEGA® Chipotle Taco Seasoning Mix.

Zesty Salads & Sides

Whole Wheat Taco Salad Bowls with Mixed Grains

MAKES 4 SERVINGS | PREP: 10 minutes **START TO FINISH:** 30 minutes

- 4 (8-inch) ORTEGA® Whole Wheat Flour Soft Tortillas
- 1 cup cooked quinoa
- 1 cup cooked barley
- ¼ cup B&G® Sliced Ripe Olives
- ¼ cup ORTEGA® Salsa, any variety
- ¼ cup fresh cilantro, chopped
- 1 tomato, diced
- 1 cup kale leaves, rinsed and thinly sliced
- 2 tablespoons olive oil
- Salt and black pepper, to taste

PREHEAT oven to 350°F.

PLACE tortillas in 4-inch baking dish; bake 15 minutes until sides of tortillas curl and create bowls.

COMBINE quinoa, barley, olives, salsa, cilantro and tomato in medium bowl; mix well. Toss in kale and oil. Add salt and pepper to taste.

SERVE mixed grain salad in baked tortilla bowls.

TIP

Garnish with toasted pecans for an added crunch.